Sea Life Mazes

Dave Phillips

DOVER PUBLICATIONS, INC.
Mineola, New York

Bibliographical Note

Sea Life Mazes is a new work, first published by Dover Publications, Inc., in 1996.

International Standard Book Number:
0-486-29422-6

Manufactured in the United States of America
Dover Publications, Inc., 31 East 2nd Street,
Mineola, N.Y. 11501

Note

Here are 46 simple mazes to tease the imagination of young readers and to teach them some amazing facts about the creatures of the sea. In each case, a fish or some other denizen of the deep is searching for a meal or its home, or hoping to find another of its kind, and you must help that creature reach its goal by completing the maze. If you get stuck, the solutions to the mazes begin on page 51.

START

FINISH

Help the emperor angelfish find its home among the coral.

This crab wants to eat the leftovers on the ocean floor.

Show the butterflyfish the way to the worms he wants for dinner.

Horseshoe crabs aren't really crabs at all, but a kind of sea spider.

7

Lionfish are beautiful, but very poisonous.
Help this one join his friends.

Leatherbacks are the largest turtles in the world. Guide this one to the squid.

START

FINISH

The coelacanth is the oldest kind of fish in the world. This one is looking for his mate.

The barracuda is fierce and fast. The little
fish will be his prey when he reaches it.

Green turtles can swim over a thousand miles.

Help the starfish find the oyster he loves to feed on.

Puffers inflate themselves like balloons when threatened. Guide this one to the coral.

Clownfish stay near poisonous sea anemones for protection.

15

Lobsters can live to be a hundred years old.

Manta rays leap into the air and come down with a loud belly flop.

17

Harp seals live on ice floats in the Arctic Ocean. Help this mother find her young one.

Pelicans collect fish in their beak pouch.
Guide bird to fish.

19

Walrus have tusks up to two feet long. Help this one get his shellfish.

Dolphins are very friendly and playful. Bring these two friends together.

21

Puffins are birds that live in Arctic waters.
Show this one the way to the fish.

Jellyfish have no brains and no bones.

Sea horses are fish that resemble horses. Get the one at the upper right to the one at the lower left.

24

START

FINISH

Penguins are birds that swim in cold waters and cannot fly. Join up these two.

Swordfish have a nose up to five feet long.

START

FINISH

Dragonfish see by a light they create with their own eyes.

START

FINISH

Linophryne are strange deep-sea fish.

Giant squid have eyes larger than those of any other creature.

The octopus has eight arms to help it catch its dinner. Lead this one to the crab.

The gigantactis attracts other fish with its own fishing rod, growing from its nose.

Sailfish have huge dorsal fins that spread out like sails.

Beluga whales live in large schools in Arctic waters. Bring these two playmates together.

Conger eels live in the waters around Europe.
Guide this one to the fish.

Gulper eels have huge mouths and catch fish in deep waters. Help this one find its prey.

Narwhals have an overgrown tooth that looks like a horn.

START

FINISH

Frill sharks are the oldest kind of shark in the world. Can this one find the fish it seeks?

Cat sharks like to eat fish, just as real cats do.

START

FINISH

Wobbegong sharks have skin with colorful patterns, like a carpet.

START

FINISH

Hammerhead sharks have heads shaped like a hammer with an eye on each end.

Goblin sharks get their name from their strange looks.

Thresher sharks use their long tails to herd fish toward each other.

Basking sharks like to float on the surface of
the sea and bask in the sun.

START

FINISH

Great white sharks are very fierce hunters.

Megamouth sharks are very rare and were only recently discovered.

START

FINISH

Whale sharks are the largest sharks, but they are very gentle.

Killer whales are friendly to people and easily tamed.

Sperm whales can swallow more than 400 pounds of food in a single gulp.

FINISH

START

Humpback whales often leap into the air, causing a great splash.

Solutions

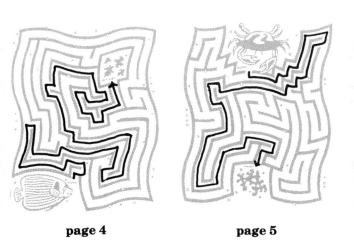

page 4   **page 5**

page 6

page 7

page 8

page 9

page 10

page 11

page 12

page 13

page 14

page 15

page 16

page 17

page 18

page 19

page 20

page 21

page 22

page 23

page 24

page 25

page 26

page 27

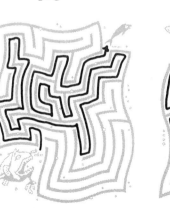

page 28

page 29

page 30

page 31

page 32

page 33

page 34

page 35

page 36

page 37

page 38

page 39

page 40

page 41

page 42

page 43

page 44

page 45

page 46

page 47

page 48

page 49